Whenever I hear something that feels like it's speaking to something that already lived inside me and I feel myself feeling 'of course' as shivers of recognition may tickle through my body.

So, my words as whispers to a wisdom that lives in you, beneath and before words. To a somatic innersense that lives under our conditioning.

So, no need to get my words with the mind, for the words are a poor translation for the subtle levels of being. The inner realms where our mythic, poetic and magical aspects form and dream reality. Our heart and belly know these places to be home despite the forgetting of our conditioned self that played the game of fitting in and yet never really forgot the Vaster Self that we are.

A call to the wisdom we knew before we learnt the words and sounds of our culture.
A call to the remember the playful mystic energy shamans we are as babies.
A call to reveal the multidimensional Soul and the Sacred Forms that live in us to be rediscovered.

So, beautiful, magnificent being don't believe anything I write or try hard to understand my words. Maybe these writings and musings like a gentle breeze blowing some dust off to reveal your own unique wisdom and seeing of the beauty of You.

No-thing to believe just your own inner wisdom being felt in the reflections of beauty you are.
I love the word Awen meaning essence, muse, flowing spirit and how we inspire each other.

Awen Benjamin

Foreword

Matthew Liam Gardner (Bruncle Bear)

I've had the honour of delivering classes and immersions all around the world. Each class and immersion is an adventure of its own kind, always as unique as the human beings who find their way into the circle.

Of all the beings that have found their way into space with me, none have quite touched my life like one particular magical, white bearded being who dresses in beautiful, colourful natural clothes, and has wonderfully wide eyes that shine with the innocence of a child, the passion of a poet and the wisdom of an ancient.

This being is called Benjamin Wallace, and he has become one of my dearest friends.

I have the honour of presenting to you a collection of Benjamin's poetry, and I find myself reflecting on the gentle yet profound impact his words have had on my own understanding and appreciation of the secret beauty that lives all around me.

Benjamin is the kind of poet who doesn't just write; he listens deeply to the undercurrents of the human experience and translates these observations and feelings they stir into verse that speaks directly to the soul.

For me, Benjamin's poetry is like a quiet but deeply moving conversation with an old wise friend.

Each line a remembering, each verse a softening.

I've had the privilege of witnessing Benjamin share his poetry more and more with our wider communities. His writing has been brewing for many years, and he has many notebooks that, over the seasons, have been filled to overflowing.

Benjamin approaches his writing with a tenderness and authenticity that is as refreshing as it is rare.

More than a collection of poems, this book captures a whisper of the great love that lives in Benjamin and the wisdom he has inherited over many years of deep listening.

Benjamin's poems are dear companions through a human life, calling us to alchemy, to beauty, and offering reflections that encourage us to look deeper, to understand more fully, and to approach our lives and the world around us with a renewed sense of care and patience.

Benjamin's poems are invitations to pause, ponder, and appreciate the richness of life.

Over the last few years, I've had the great honour and the joy of spending quite a lot of time with Benjamin, though not nearly enough, and together with our dear brother Alastair Cuthbert, we've explored, deepened, and grown together.

Along the way, we've shared our poetry, our listenings, and our rememberings with each other, and this shared dreaming space has culminated in the birthing and rising of the School of Living Myth - An international Wisdom School that's breathing deep listening and deep humanity back into our world.

I will forever be grateful for Benjamin's whispers, for his poetry, and for his unique form of love in dreaming this school into existence.

As you turn the pages of this book in your hands, you will no doubt find yourself returning to certain lines or poems, discovering new layers of meaning with each visit.

This is the gift of Benjamin's poetry – it grows with you, offering new revelations and inspirations as you journey ever deeper.

It is my hope that this book becomes a cherished companion of yours and that it finds its way into many hands and hearts.

It is my honour to introduce you to the poetry of Benjamin Wallace.

Matthew Liam Gardner. An Australian-born Embodiment Teacher, and something like an Emerging Elder of the Western World, now living in the foothills of the Black Mountains in Wales

To learn more about our school, you can visit:
www.schooloflivingmyth.com

Foreword

Alastair Cuthbert (Bruncle Polar Bear)

I am deeply honoured to be asked to contribute to this wonderful book, having met Benjamin a few years back around the mid-point of my journey to fully feeling what it is to be a whole being in the world today.
It also helped that our beards and wardrobes were in some spiritual synchronicity.
Benjamin's medicine is truly unique, of all the wonderful teachers, guides and medicine I have encountered, Benjamin's has had the most significant impression on me.
We have attended countless workshops and retreats together, travelling many hours across the country - we have had so many wonderful adventures!
Our conversations are always mind expanding and soul nourishing - I felt that I frequently arrived with more Gold from the conversation to the retreat than most would leave with, likewise the journey home always felt like a personalised integration session. This was truly a golden age for me, for along with the belly wisdom our Dear Brother and

Uncle Matthew Liam Gardener brought to our lives this became the most enlivening, educational and embodied time of my existence.

I vividly recall sitting in a tent with Benjamin in a magical Welsh Valley, experiencing the immensity of feeling within as the numbness fell away from my heart and my very being continued to open wider, wider, ever wider.
I was deeply afraid.
Scared in truth by the raging river of discomforting feelings that I was sure would drown or overwhelm my being. Benjamin posed the question 'What if it is the rise of the feminine energy - the feelingness - inside your being that you are experiencing?'
This was a profound gift for my development, as I sank into the deep mystery, I found a wholeness and balance that I cherish. The journey to feeling continues with that foundation to this day.

The magical prose contained in this book takes me back - indeed it gives a real feeling of the conversations Benjamin, Matthew and I have enjoyed.
It is my sincere wish that you, the reader will come to see them as a true gift to your soul - as they have been for mine.

Thank you Benjamin, for your teaching, your brotherhood, your humanity. For showing me what it truly is to be a Brother, a Man, a Human Being in this time, in this world.
For sharing the Love that you are, I love you Benjamin, your presence and grace have ever been a gift to my being.

Sacred Wound

We all feel wounded, broken, fractured, separated from source, from our Okness. So much of our psyche is built on avoiding and protecting that vulnerability that was too much for our young systems to process.

Maybe each of us have a unique flavour to that wound - I am not good enough, I am all alone, it's all my fault, I am unlovable, I will be abandoned etc. probably a combination of many. Mine is I am wrong, not for anything in particular, even though I spent years searching for what I may have done wrong in this life and past life.

There is a medicine within the wound, like the antidote to the snake bite in its tail

(not sure if this just folklore, but I like the metaphor).
The medicine of the wound, when we turn towards it and sit with it as a loving parent is an initiation, a portal, a womb into rebirthing our wholeness. A remembering of our innocence and our wholeness.

The fracturing isn't just our wound, its ancestral wounding that has been passed down the generations. The patriarchal culture and that turned away from the earth as Goddess.

A split between mind and nature, where the conditioned mind in its protection forgot the innersence of nature to which it is guardian. The outer levels of awareness running up and away from the earth of our bodies, the outer forgetting that it is in service and devotion to the inner levels of beingness.

But like a wave never can never really be separate from the Ocean even when it thinks it is. And a sound never separate from the silence from which it arose.
There is a call to turn towards our wounding as a loving parent to a child, to give her the loving boundaries and offer the loving words and actions that the young ones never received.
And we in our wholeness get to be the one relearning how to be the elder we never had and the young one being reparented and the subtle loving mother holding all from within.
And noticing in my own system if I only have access one aspect, I end up in a co-

dependent game with outside, until I am able to embrace that aspect as well.

For example, being in my vulnerability and feeling like outside is judging me, where I am seeing others as critical parents through the lens of my inner critic. As I face my own inner critic and bring him into alignment, I rediscover within him is the emerging lion learning he is in service to my innocence. He was never given the space to have his No and boundaries honoured as sacred. I saw distortions of his strong energy outside and I avoided him and made him bad, his assertiveness. So, he ended up protecting by throwing the blame at self or others, either way his system was feeling the pain of the blame.

The other side is where I am in my strong parental energy without access to my own innocence. So rescuing, caretaking or controlling other's feelings and nervous systems. Rather than my own nervous system and feelings being my primary beloved.

Whenever we are out of balance throwing an unowned part outside, the universe acts like a pendulum calling these parts to be honoured.
The mind and the subtle within learning they are lovers.

*Holding the child that feels wrong
with or without a story,
softening
into
the womb of being,
with father's face
offering blessings,
kissing the wound
within
the protection
of the judge,
holding fear with courage,
sitting
in the
sacred wound
the womb
the portal of innersense and grace*

So many stories
Ancestral wounds and blessings
Tails and Myths waiting to be felt
Why do we keep telling the same stories?
Inherited stories that don't seem to serve
Overwhelming moment from our past, held as cellular memories
Children waiting for a cuddle
Waiting for their sacred forms to be revealed
Waiting to be met, to be embodied
to be heard, to be dreamed into their sacred forms that they have always been,
Sleeping mountains
Pregnant Nebulas birthing the Mythic

Each Sacred form in Devotion to
the Ocean that hears All
Each story a Myth
Each curse the medicine and
blessing
When fully digested
Space for new ancient dreamings
Space for a cat to curl up in the
golden sunshine
Space for a phoenix to dance on
silver moonbeams

All as Beloved

Sitting with the sacred wounds and when they feel safe and honoured, they reveal the innocence that lives within them. The innersense that they have always been like a seed in the sacred ground of our being. Learning to turn towards all aspects, as a new-born baby, with that same reverence and gratitude for the grace that they hold, for the grace from which all is born.

When I don't speak to an aspect with respect for it's innocence, it appears to be other than it's sacred nature.

This present moment is like the Mother in her loving Is-ness, holding from within.

She holds this precious new-born moment from within. As Awe-are-ness acts as Father learning to bless from above the beautiful one in its wide-open innocence.

So many aspects of our being we are conditioned to turned away from, the labels they are given have so much baggage that it obscures our clear seeing of their beauty.

It is not the aspect of our psyche that are a problem it is our ideas and opinions about them that tarnish our relationship to them, our intimacy with them.
These aspects must contort and to shout to get the love and recognition they need, so much that their true essence and forms are hard to distinguish.

So, when we say use words like fear, anger, darkness, mind, death, life, love, ego, desire, surrender, sensuality, ego or whatever we are not talking about their essence or sacred forms. We are talking about our ideas and relationship to those ideas, our relationship to the words.
When we start relating to all aspects as beloved, we clear our relationship to their essence within and start to reclaim our words.

Deep down I remember I don't know anything, that I know nothing and
I am no-thing. In that willingness to dissolve into the formless we are able to dance in the knowing, in the different forms that come ago.
That beautiful I Don't Know is the Beloved hidden within all forms, under all words.

She is the Great Mystery, the formless beauty from which all beauty and visions of beauty arise.
I love remembering that I love the Beloved, the Ocean of Devotion that moves all - the stars radiating, the atoms dancing, the ideas blossoming, the bees pollinating, the heart beating, this whole mysterious happening.

So, a call for us to turn toward all within and around as the Beloved being born. As we remember we are both the beloved and the lover being initiated. The toddler and the master being initiated.
The Acorn and the Mighty Oak.

As I turn toward that which I was told to turn away from, I feel each word fear, anger, death, mind was just another name for love.

As I bring love to my fear, to my shyness I feel the love that they have always been. As I turn to Death as my Beloved, I feel her as my loving Mother, the Sacred Darkness and the Mystery of Love that is my being. The subtle mother birthing Yoni-verses and songs, dreaming all of life, from her liminal belly.

We are taught to turn away from death, from being, from peace and from the Isness of things, from the subtle into the loud.

We live in a culture running from being into doings as an avoidance.

Avoidance of the Isness, of the deep feminine. We are running from the sacred ground of death that holds us.

Death births all of life and is the womb from which all comes and returns to and never really leaves. Doings, dreamings and sounds are beautiful when arising from a reverence of the Silence rather than a separation from her.

Thank you thoughts
I am sorry I thought you were wrong
I am done fighting with you
You are welcome to be part of this whole symphony
I feel your hidden devotion to the silence
Doing in loving service to deep Beingness
Welcome to this haven of love we are

Meeting you afresh

each moment

the vulnerability of feeling

through each form

into the mirror

of your open heart and my open heart

this holy place

before the stars and universe were birthed

Sitting between death and birth

in silent reverence,

pregnant moment

stillness moving the Yoni-verse

Tears filling up dry eyes

Heart fluttering.

A place we deeply know before unknown

became words

I'm done chasing reflections of you Beloved,

outside of myself

Closer than the breath

Closer than sound and the words they form

For you Beloved Silence,

pregnant with every sound in swirling

ecstasy

The place before place is born

I digress entranced by your wisdom by your

Love

I'm done seeking you outside

Waiting for some perfect reflection before a

bow and dissolve

"I" is learning that he has always been in

devotion to you

Learning to be the lover he's always been to

you Beloved One

As I taste you within in; dissolve as you, you

revealed yourself in all forms

Hiding within so I don't get distracted by

your outside costumes

You've always been waiting in your

nakedness calling me home to ourself

Into the intimacy of our aloneness where all

beings reside in

Sweet Harmony

Aloneness the Sacred Ground from
which You and I arise,
O Beloved One
the aloneness
of you
in your naked Mystery,
when all your garments have
dissolved into your beauty,

In the Silence before words were
birthed,

Before I thought self and other were
two,
When even one was too many,
O beloved all-one-ness may I hold
you close like the new-born baby you
are,
No longer

running from you beloved
trying to find
you
in another,
When I meet you
within
I dissolves
in sweet devotion
and I met you everywhere and
nowhere,
O Beloved Ocean of my Soul each
wave a celebration of your mystery.
You are my mother, father and my
child,
The sacred womb from which they
come,
All names are yours, formed from
your Silence.

Wild tenderness with this
moment,
Abandoned
Alone
Dying and Born anew at
same time,
Without meaning and full of
reverence,
Being Love
before
need to give or receive
in its
ripe emptiness.

Love before she had a name,
touching all as Beloved without
need to change even a speck

of dust as it glistens in the

sunlight of its own nature

held the womb of its own

Darkness

The Beautiful
I Don't Know

If we look at what we know, we realise that we truly know nothing.
But there is a vulnerability walking around in a world, a culture that pretends it knows. Deep down in our heart, in our belly and even our mind we feel we know nothing truly. That this whole existence is a Great Mystery, that we put labels on then sit in our ivory towers pretend we know and all is safe and rational.

When I look at any word surrender, love, death, mind feelings, good, bad, even though I can give a dictionary definition, I know I don't really know what they mean. In that not knowing there is a beauty a realising no one knows, so there is space to play, space to dream. Space to play in the mystery, the mystic.

The beautiful I don't know, the place of innersense, of feelingness, of love's mysterious wisdom. Space to dance, dream, play, romance the earth. Underneath the world, our culture is the vast wisdom of the earth, of our bodies. Unfathomable by the knowing of our minds, which are vessels for the deeper wisdom that grows oak trees, pollinates flowers and spins galaxies.

So, the beautiful I Don't Know bowing to the heart that allows waves of knowing and seeing of beauty to arise to the mind and fall back to the belly.

Moving from a ridged attitudes to words pointing at things to befriending our relationship to the words so we can be in intimacy with the essence underneath. Under the stories, words and forms is the beloved innocence we never left, being in intimacy with our roots. When the witnesser is able to soften into intimacy with the experiencer within, we move from objectifying the earth to Inner Alchemy of Love.

The word earth has the word ear within it to remind us of the deep listening that we are born from. Also earth has the word art within to remind us we are art we don't need to try to be beautiful we already are.

At the Temple gates of the Great Mystery
I offer my knowing,
dissolving into my body of unknowing,
the Blessings of my knowings,
a key of light,
to enter her Wholly Darkness,
sometimes just
the
gentle
thought
of
"it's safe to drop,
to dissolve,
to soften,
to die"
"It's safe not to know"
"It's safe to forget"
......

I drop into
the body of forgiveness,
of Sacred receptivity,
As I drop and soften
knowings and memories
arise,
like twinkling stars,
sometimes I follow them out,
forgetting
I am the space
I am safe
I am worthy just to be,
a running
from
the Temple of Now and Here,
of no-where
into somewhere,
into doing,
into future promises of a
better now,
this Present Mama is
forgiveness

a continual
seat
a haven
to rest
into,
her subtle waters nourishing
all,
to willingly surrendering
my concepts,
to this loving presence,
already held,
the depths of the Ocean
allowing and blessed
by the waves on the surface,
waves in unknown devotion
to their depths,
stars dancing in the night
sky swirling in love,
imaginings in liminal
innersense,
sublime kissing the subtle,

Light is a mirror to the
Unseen Beauty of the
Darkness,
a tree already in an acorn,
Father time looking back
through
Mother space
to see how his Sacred Form
was birthed

Where do my words come from?
I don't know,
How comes I don't lose the
thread in my speaking?
Its deeper than the words,
arising from the belly of
unknowing,
I don't even know who is
speaking,
There is some subtle tuning into
some feelingness then a
translating,
Is the mind just a translator?
An artist translating some vast
beauty unfathomable,
If I am not who I think I Am
who Am I?

Mmmm Oooo Aaaaa ....
Am I willing to dissolve and reform a thousand times?
To unknow myself,
Do I have a choice?
The choiceless choice?
An alignment to what already is happening,
To be the no-thing birthing every-thing,
all things falling back into Am-ness,
into Mothers loving embrace,
How to I speak?
How to I do anything?
A playfully constructed idea of I,

As if the wave could be
anything but the loving
happening-ness of the Ocean,
Moving all from a place of not
moving, of stillness,
of silence singing creation
awake
and
a lullaby back to rest,
Seasons of love turning the
spiral wheel,
Yearning to tenderly caress a
string within in that resonates
in another's being,
To play a chord in the subtlety
of my inner temple of space,

So that the somatic wisdom of
Silence shimmers and smiles,
The unknowing before words
and forms became known,
Deep So-Ma, Mother of all,
In her deep dark waters sublime
water vapours arise skyward,
Sweet tears as awe-ness softens
back through the body,
With blessings of liquid light
kissing every cell, every fibre in
a static Union.
A Union, a Loving that's always
been,
Oh, Beloved Ocean as sky my
tears fall back to you,

Oh, Sky Seeing One, my lover, caress me as Ocean with your Divine remembrance, Remembrance of Sacred Nature, Mmm Sweet Silence pregnant with every knowing that will ever be birthed, every sound, every light in your eternal Womb.

The beautiful I don't know
is the one who experiences all
so even though I don't know
I still
whisper
to the Great Mystery
of
I don't know that is my belly
the beautiful no-thing
into which
my identities dissolve
and
from
which
everything is born
and
really there is no 'thing'
no separation
between object and observer

no separation
between sound
and the silence that hears

no separation

between my knowing
and my not knowing

no separation
between awareness
and beingness

my knowing
is like
the protective surface
of the
bubble around
the tenderness
of I don't know

The holy darkness
the womb of creation
birthing the light of each form
like a wave on her ocean

The wound of creation
really the womb of creation
when gently turned towards
with reverence

Beauty Under

In our search for knowing and safety we go up and out, leave our bodies leave home. Want to be up, happy, in the light, in pure awareness. All of this is fine to get a bit of perspective, but we can't live on the mountain top. Spiritual practises that try this are part of the old paradigm a patriarchal avoidance of nature, of seasons, of feelings and of the body.
And they don't work.
They are an unfaced trauma response playing out.
How about we turn things on their head and recognise all that we are searching for is under and within. Source is not up and far away in the sky in as distance God, a Far-ther separate from us.

As we drop down into safety, into relaxed nervous system into soft belly all we search for is subtly resting here in her mystery, in Deeper Self, our Okness.
All the knowings already here in the beautiful I don't know in the Yes of Being.

Maybe as realisations arise, we think where we became aware of them is where they come from. So, we think ideas come from the head, unaware that all arises from the subtle feelingness of the vast wisdom of the earth of our body. The earth under the earth. Like a sound, all its wisdom and love are a manifestation of that which lives within the silence, a wave on her deep Ocean.

The mysterious beauty of our beingness

The innersense of the one who experiences all

The openness that feels all

All different names to the one who feels can call the Mystery – Her,
Love,
Peace,
Is-ness,
Beloved,
Me (Mother in Everything)
Our nakedness before we started to wear forms.

There are lots of practises about becoming the witnesser, being pure awareness, which is beautiful, yet is missing the beloved, the experiencer within. The witnesser without its beloved is co-dependent with life, constantly seeking for its own centre outside of itself. We see this in our culture that gives rise to the immature masculine that is abusive to the innocence. Our culture even puts on a pedestal the transcendent aspect and disconnects from the experiencer, from the earth, from our Wholly nature.

Each of the seasons has its unique medicine, a tree's branches as needed as the roots. Our culture is calling for its own roots, its own forgotten beauty and innocence. The branches on their own cant dream, for it is the earth and the roots dreaming through the trunk and branches.

When channelling or tuning into the akashic often people speak as if from above in a far way dimension. Which is

one way, but it fosters a sense of separation. More beautiful is to tune into them being under and within. So, when we are channelling, we can allow aspects of the vaster being that we all are through. A willingness to drop down into the subtle realms of our being.
It may be that we become aware of the different forms and expressions as they rise to the surface. But let's not confuse where they come from.

Also, I am tired the of demonising of down, the feminine, darkness, feelings, bodies, sensuality.
Which is really turning away from stillness and beingness at the heart of doings and things. And when we make any feeling wrong and run away into the mind, we automatically feel the mind is

also bad. So, when we make the feminine wrong and run to the safety of the masculine, the masculine also then feels wrong disconnected from its roots. When we don't bless the experiencer and run to just being the witnesser there is a fracturing.

The experiencer as a newborn that needs reminding of its innate worthiness and guiding into revealing its sacred forms and the witnesser mirroring back the love like an emerging elder.

There are many stories and experiences that have not been fully digested individually and as a culture. Part of the digesting is feeling the innocence that lives within all stories. The witnesser can be a loving father reminding the innocence of its original nature and beauty.

I keep falling through
things
because
I am not a thing
and
I start to remember
from
my
perspective
things
are arising through me

Speaking to the One who
digests,
The One who listens,
intimacy with her
the spacious emptiness,
each form
speaking to her Mystery,

Sacred forms polished
in the
fathomless depths
this moment,
intimacy of each form with
its mother,
a deepening
of its devotion
as
the snake's skins unfolds

Aho Beloved how can it be that I feel your words flow through a poet's words,
And other times they are lost in translation,
I feel you whisper and sometimes shout within me "those are second hand words",
"They do not honour my fullness and my emptiness in equal measure,
Why do I fly in the sky grasping some stability when You are equally in the depths,
You do not exclude any,

You say "don't speak words as if the came directly from my lips, from my belly unless they embrace all as I do,"
For Your song is a free as the birdsong, the smile of a baby, a dewdrop on a blade of grass and hidden even in the words of a liar,
For what is there to lie about other that I Am already here awaiting you as you,
There is a time and place and an eloquence in how and when to speak the beauty,

I say beauty for the word truth has been hijacked by linear thinking,
You whisper "I can never fully be expressed by a line, when I Am a circle, a spiral, a messy squiggle. My beauty is expressed differently through words and actions through a warrior, to a gardener, to a mother, to a child, to a father. And all of them feel me uniquely. And I give each a different medicine to carry. Although secretly my medicine under all medicine is available to

all, by virtue and by grace of your very being.

There is a holy shyness that saves my deepest medicine's expressions for the quietest and subtlest of times. Then my sublime blessings flow as if not from here or there and not from now or then. For time and space arise from my dreaming belly, just as you and I. And we are much more intimate that that my lover. For lover and beloved are ripples in my deep ocean."

Alchemy

of

Mother and Father

The Peruvian Quechua language has the same word for fight as dance when it comes to opposite energies.

So, we can carry on the imagined fracturing between dark and light, down and up, mind and feelings, joy and sadness, anger and fear, strong and soft, self and other.

Or we can come to remember they are dancing together, making love.

The top and bottom of the breath make love and support each other. The bottom of the breath softening into

beingness into the body and the formlessness within, the depths of the ocean.
The top of the breath lightening into Awe-are-ness, the seeing of the beauty that lives in the depths and reveals itself as we fill up with breath, a blossoming.
Breath is another word for love.

The breath shows us the play, the lovemaking of experiencer and witnesser. How like the Yin Yang symbol they flow into and become each other, never really two separate things.
As we fill up with breath, with our inbreath, our up breath, the experiencer starts to become conscious of herself and become the witnesser. As we empty down soften with our 'out' breath, the

down breath, the witnesser softens into and becomes the experiencer.
The breath is the love between beingness and awe-are-ness.

When using the words masculine and feminine there can be a confusion and mistakenly using them to mean male and female. We can use Yang and Yin, sun and moon, expressive and receptive which help tune into the essences under the words.
I feel it is important to reclaim our somatic understanding of these words masculine and feminine.
That these essences live in all beings male, female, trees, stones, animals.
So essential I am referring to the receptivity and the expressiveness and how they dance together like the breath

and the seasons. And really could not be separate as they dream each other into being with their love.

The fracturing comes when we just want one side of the breath, just want one season we automatic create an imbalance.

In that only having one side, we throw the other side outside until we can learn to embrace it in our wholeness. We are not just co-dependent with a partner or friend we are co-dependent with life.

The pinch of our co-dependence teaching us our interdependence, each from and expression and essential ingredient to the whole cosmic soup.

And life is continually inviting us into our wholeness.

Into the alchemical union of beingness and awareness in the heart, like the trunk of the tree patiently waiting and being a bridge between heavens and earth. The rainbow bridge of our spine, our chakras. Beloved kundalini serpent sensually dancing within the tree of life, to the music of the yoni-Verses.

The words Mother and Father need blessing and digesting so we can attune to their true essences and be able to embody both. At different times I maybe more in one than the other. I used to think that the only way I could be in my tenderness or feeling was to throw my mind away. That the only way to be with my inner child was to abandon having an inner father, then left hypersensitive and being on the check to see if another was being an aligned father or not. So, learning that I can be in my child with my own inner father available and then better able to allow others to hold me.

Really my inner father is the filter through which other's father comes, if my inner father is in critic mode that is all he will hear from outside. And conversely when my inner father is aligned his heart's discernment can see another's blame or criticism is about their view of life of their own innocence. When the father's sacred protection and guardianship is to the subtle beauty within, he can see this innocence lives in all forms.

Each person's face, movement and voice showing me where they are at with the Alchemy of their masculine and feminine,

their spirit and soul, their witnesser romancing their experiencer.
How their head is talking to their belly, how lovingly they talk to their body and the innersense within.

I can only be my experiencer even though it is the same subtle One experiencing within all.
I can only attune to my witnesser's seeing. Alchemy of my light loving my holy darkness, my seeing and hearing romancing each other.
My I-magic-nation learning to speak to the mystery within.

One Is-ness , One Heart, One Seeing.
    Belly   **Heart**   **Mind**
Sometimes being more in my inner feminine other times more in my inner

masculine. Both coming into alignment attunement harmony when have each other available within.

So many words to play with for these lovers-
Father/Mother,
Light/Darkness,
Sound/Silence,
Sublime/Subtle,
Spirit/Soul,
Witnesser/Experiencer,
Doing/Being,
Will/Surrender,
Giving/Receiving,
Head/Belly,
Up/Down,
Expressive/Receptive,
Talking/Hearing.

All polarities as a Yang and a Yin.
All in this cosmic lovemaking.

The baby, our innersense lives in our belly deeply connected, one with all. The belly of Mother, deep beingness, relaxed nervous system.

The spine, our backbone, the tree of life travels up to the face, the mask-uline, the awe-are-ness, the outer forms their surface and boundaries.

The heart is the meeting place, the holy temple of their eternal union, already wedded here. The Love between the Father and Mother flows through the child, the innocence, the heart of all.

An Ancient dance
older than the stars
younger than this new-born
moment,
Between
Awe-ness and Is-ness,
Between them the love
the devotion
the fabric of creation,
The devotion of my
remembering to my
forgettings,
eternal lovers,
All polarities in a dance and
alchemical union,
a reflection
of the creativity of love

All forms blessing the
formless the sacred void,
The sovereign king reborn
from his sacrificial death

Born of the grace of the virgin space,
The Soul beneath the Soil,
A willingness to die into this moment,
In each breath a reflection of this great surrender to love,
Of the holding of awe-ness to be willing to soften into her womb,
The spiral galaxies weaving their magic,
Blessings rippling through the fabric of space and time,
Ripples in her Ocean,
The nameless One to whom in my unknowings and subtle knowings,
I have always been devoted to

To move in this world as the
blessings we are,
just by grace of our being,
Each breath love in action
blessing each cell of creation

The artists always expressing the inexpressible back to the mystery,
Life praising its source,
Words expressing the unspeakable back to the silence,
Sounds romancing the silence,
Forms kissing the Formless,
Sky hugging the Earth,
Cosmic Father loving Divine Mother of All,
I Am dancing on that rainbow bridge held in their loving union,
Radiant light of love returning to luscious womb of creation,
to dance it's spiral dance again,
with each breath,
with each heartbeat of ma-tter,

Sacred Forms

Forms identities, waves on the ocean. We can get fixed on one form to the exclusion of all others. This is who I am. Maybe of fixation on one particular form is based more on our avoidance of another.
Avoidance of death, of being, of anger, of not belonging, of being stupid, of being weak, of being strong, of being like our parents or those who hurt us.

Turning towards, a willingness to welcome home all aspects of ourselves. To the holy ground which they never left, our wholeness.
All forms are sacred arisings, birthed from the sensual sacral-ness of love. The

space from which these waves of forms dance. So, if all forms are sacred maybe it is just our turning aways from them that make them contort and appear to be less than holy. They are waiting for us to look them straight in the eye, to feel them in the belly and behold them in the heart.

Like sound and silence, they are not two opposite 'things' there is a gradual whispering as silence expresses itself as sound. The subtle inner planes arising into forms.
These subtle forms that live inside us, gently sleeping in the subtle realms of the Great Mother, in our bellies. They live in the deep listening, in the dreaming. As we feel into these forms and dreamings we bring them forth and reveal them, the forms become more tangible. Even in

their tangibility they get their sustenance from their roots from the Subtle Isness - from Death.

We can often think of death as against life. But what if death is just who we are before we took on forms, the mystery of Am-ness. What would it be like if we saw death as our original nature our innocence as the home from which we dream this multiverse of forms. The Sacred Darkness dreaming all the forms and light and stars and galaxies and atoms just to bless her unfathomable beauty.

This sacred darkeness is the subtle the birthplace of the mythic, the mystic Mama.

Within each of us exist a multitude of sacred forms and mythical aspects and we secretly and subtly know these to also be who we are.

As we start to acknowledge these aspects and dreamings that live in us we give permission for other to reveal who they truly are.

Often, we walk around holding back from acknowledging love are all are until others reveal it. Or waiting of the one person that we are reserving that love for, then when they come, we are not very practised in just Being the love. We can easily think that the love was cause by outside then attempt to control outside to grasp an outside reflection.

My muse the sacred
formless One,
birther of all forms,
to which
each form
is truly devoted,
as they reveal
the master
they have always been,
as I soften into
my
devotion,
I see you
in all
and
abide
as
you

Our Sacred Forms are a secret
an open secret,
only in our Innocence
can we feel and see their presence,
the Mystic Innocence of our Being,
when I
recognise we all live here,
I more gracefully abide here,
when
I try to cast another from this garden,
it is myself that imagines itself abandoned,

softly
resting
into
the
Holy Cave of Solitude,
remembering
the sacred aloneness in All,
Beloved Oceanic One,
my Sacred Muse,
Birther of Yoni-Verses

forms as sacred
as
the space that holds them,
flowers blossoming,
an
expression of
the sacred darkness,
their fragrance
romancing
the bees
to drink their golden nectar
of life,
whispers
intimate
with the
silence

The dance of the mythic,
this mythic landscape is home,
the home we never left,
from where do we experience this sensual life,
the sensual mystic underbelly of life,
call her womb of creation,
oceanic sensual muse within all,
Call her beloved,
death,
Life

sacred void,
quantum field,
Call her me, you, love,
peace
Call her what you want,
this is not her true
name,
names are like clothes
on our primordial
nakedness,
somewhere deep within
before words and
images arose,
before knowing arose,
before remembering,
there was,
Or rather there IS,

And I love you,
beautiful mysterious
muse in all your
costumes

Approval and Disapproval

We were brought up with reward and punishment.
Told that we are good or bad depending on if we met the expectations of our parents or teachers conditioning.
We are born into in a culture of making things good or bad.
Shamed into behaving certain pre-conceived ways.
Then we carry on that way of parenting ourselves, of fathering ourselves. I say fathering, because it is more of the father principle in both men and women that holds the structures and boundaries.
How I treat other reflects how I treat that aspect of myself and vice versa. So, we are relearning how to speak and act to

ourselves, to reparent ourselves. To reparent the innocence within, the way it was never fully met and loved.
Our subconscious doesn't know the difference between something we say to someone else or to ourselves. So, when we blame or judge another it feels like it was us that was getting it wrong. Our body feels as if we were judged blamed or told off.

What if there was no one left to blame including myself.
There is a medicine in blame - my fire, my assertiveness, my core-rage, my anger for me, a loving strong boundary for me. Maybe I blame because I feel I am not allowed that energy. Not allowed to have a loving strong father within.

Often, we either have absent father principle or the opposite of a strict disciplinarian. And an oscillation between the two.

I am liking the words 'devoted father' which speak to the father principle that can hear and validate feelings and impulses and hold loving boundaries and guidance that doesn't need to shame. When the strong father is allowed to be for me, to come from my heart, he can hold loving boundaries and sacred protection and reverence for the innersense within.

We can project our conditioning, our ideas of reward and punishment onto the world. Basically, projecting out our inner critic onto the world. Hidden in the conditioning of the inner critic is the

devoted father, when we feel resourced enough to meet the young masculine protection disguised as the inner critic. Our devoted father as our inner champion.
Learning how to guide the innersense that lives within to be able to say no to a pattern or behaviours whilst big yes and validation to all the feelings.
How often are we rebelling with an aspect outside that we have not come into attunement within. This can be authority father principle or the wildness, nature, freedom, innocence.

So, a call to recognising the universe is not rewarding and punishing us for behaviours, feelings and thoughts. It is just through the filter of our immature father that we perceive it as such. We are clearing for the collective the idea that we need or deserve to be punished or rewarded to conform, that there is something wrong with our nature. A shift from original sin to Original Blessing, as if our true nature could anything but a miraculous Mystery and Grace.

The immature masculine in culture shifting to be the inner champion and custodian of nature.

Hidden within our blame is our emerging Lion finding its place as guardian to our innocence. Even within our inner critic is the core-rage that didn't know the sacred ground of beingness which it serves.

As we learn to meet our feelings in the subtle, before they have to search for a story or reason to justify their existence.

Before they had to search of an outside cause or label, we met them in the emotional oneness of the Subtle Mother of All.
Then their true forms as flavours of love in devotion to the beloved within can more readily be revealed.

Forgiveness
is my calm nervous system
the centre of the wheel
blessed
by all the seasons
of the nervous system
I eye in devotion to the
spiral galaxy
the Space blossoming it's
Sacred Fragrance

I read words of precision,
Do I feel them as refined Petals of
Devotion,
Honey dripping down my spine,
or
As cleverness proving it's worth,
Arrows seeking a target.
Running from the mystery of not knowing
Rising away from the beauty of being, of
feeling.
The same wound of unworthiness,
the subtle turning towards,
leaning into the sacred wound,
the womb.
Does my head in its protection,
forget who it serves,
The knowing in devotion to the Great
Unknowing,
The words golden honeycombs of Silence,
How could a wave ever be other than the
oceanic mother.
Can my masculine armour soften into Amor
with the Beloved feminine,
Strength from my tenderness,

Safe to softening with my boundaries and sacred forms holding space,
Is it safe for me to hear your words and not understand?
Do they demand I come up to meet them
or
Do they soften down to meet me as a falling feather,
Do they demand they are right and light and push against wrong and mystery and tenderness and darkness,
As I digest my own knowing and my words there is a sacred Alchemy and meeting the heart of the matter.
A Devotion of my Mind of light to my Beloved Ocean of Soul.
My face kissing the Belly of Creation in Sweet Reverence.

What do we doubt in self-doubt?
Just ideas about ourselves,
but we are not an idea or a concept,
So, what if we allowed ourselves to fully
doubt everything we were told about
ourselves that doesn't resonate in our
heart and belly,
Followed doubt all the
way into the mystery of feelingess,
all the way home into
the beautiful I don't know,
Like sadness allowed to wash us clean
down into our naked true nature,
What if each emotion that rose didn't
really want to justify its existence on
some outside reason,
some outside cause,

What if each emotion
was calling
for our
awe to
witness them
in their
wild innersense
before they had to shout and
contort to get our at-tension or

create a

story to be heard

What if ?

Already

Underneath
the Drama
of my Karma
is the Dharma
of my True Nature

Four Angels

As we learn to meet fear, anger, sadness, joy and peace in the subtle before words. We feel them as flavour of love, sacred seasons of the heart. Each with its unique flavour and gift.

In each of the four directions

the **angel of earth** – Winter
    fear, shyness, awe, excitement

the **angel of fire** – Spring
    anger, spontaneity, assertiveness,

the **angel of air** – Summer
    joy, clarity, blossoming, blessing

the **angel of water** – Autumn
        sadness, forgiveness, softening

and

  in the centre -Home
        the angel of peace - subtle, Isness

As we learn to bow to these angels as our children, as our beloved, as our teachers and guardian. We clear their names.

The four chambers of the heart already dancing in beauty, in love romanced by the breath. The seasons turning in their spiral dance.

The breath gently meets all before words and brings whatever is ready up into the light of awe-are-ness.

From the subtle up into the sublime, each breath a refinement a blossoming offering itself back down into the body and the subtle within with blessings.

Wanting to speak to the sacredness that is fear. Because it feels it is the first one to be excluded. Cast out from love.

Don't be frightened, there is nothing to be frightened of, don't be coward.
We carry on this shaming of fear in our spirituality - its low vibe, fear-based thoughts, choose love not fear.

How abouts we chose to love fear or at least love the frightened one. I am learning to bring love to fear before it

needs to shout and is overwhelming to my nervous system.
As I learn to bless the subtle whispers of fear, of shyness, I feel fear as the sensual love. It is the openness of feelingness before it got the label fear and was shamed.

When I have welcomed fear, I have felt safe, no longer anything to run from. No longer needing any reason to justify why I feel fear, so no longer things making me frighted. Just fear as the tenderness of love holding me, as the excitement of my beingness.
It is only in my rising above turning away from fear that make me feel unsafe. In the willingness to be with the sacred feeling called fear there is a willingness to meet all the other flavour of love.

For when I cast out fear all the other flavours of love, there true forms were also forgotten.

There is medicine, a love, a sacred essence that lives in each feeling, each form, each thought, each movement and each sound. Learning to meet each in the subtle before words and curses were layered on top, as we met them here in the grace of the present mama their true forms are revealed. In the wholly womb of creation her gratitude births each form as a blessing. Softening into relationship and intimacy with each flavour of Love.

Throughout my body
within every cell,
is an ocean of sadness
an ocean of forgiveness,
connecting the
surface
of
my
mind
to
the depth of my bones,
a sadness connecting all,
a love connecting all,
sacred seasons of love,
waves of thoughts arise,
as do sensations
and feelings,
and their natural falling,
a softening into my being,
into
this ocean of love,

my
awareness
softening
into body,
into
the heart of matter,
this sweet sadness softening,
into
the sacred
sacral,
womb of creation,
into the mystery,
into the not knowing,
into feelingness,
continually softening down,
with gravity,
a receiving
be-fore-giving,
my mind's memories of
distrust of the down,
holding onto up,

as if my own mother was
other
than
the sacredness of death
continually
rebirthing me,
beautiful sadness anger fear
& joy,
you are the medicine itself,
that clears your names,
the subtle feeling of you
in your whispers,
before labels
and
before you needed
to distort yourself to be
heard,
after knowing
you in your nakedness,
in your subtle innocence,
as the love you are,
and then hearing you as love

even the times you've needed
to shout,
even in your sacred purge
your essence once felt
cannot be unfelt

No need to get over my fear, bypass or transend my fear. No need to try to be fearless.

Having the courage to love the frightened One,
to recognise the angel hidden within that which hasn't been loved.
The innersense that we have always been.
As we love and hold the frightened One we begin to recognise all the feelings as flavours of love

Tiredness
    sadness
        forgetfulness
            grief
                forgiveness
each word
    a whisper
 for the dropping down
            into
    I don't know
        the beautiful I don't know
            that is feelingness
this dropping down
    to the dark mystery of the Heart
        of the Belly
            the Soul

 maybe each dropping down
            a death
        a softening of identities
        a dissolving of ego
        a dissolving of patterns
    like sleep there's a moment
                of
            Surrender

   at
      the
          bottom
              of
                the
                    Breath
where I dissolve
        into nature

     where all doing
         all ideas
            all visions of Beauty
are placed
    at the altar
        of the Present Mama
in her vast belly
    is the unborn Innocence
        of who we are
under all our ages
      all our costumes
    all our forms
the formless Innocence
  of the Most Beautiful One
the Deep Ocean
            the Womb of Creation

    as
        I soften
            into the sacred wound
                turn towards the fracturing
                    the seperation
I become
    or
        more I rest
      in the still point
    that is everywhere and now.here
      this present moment
      simultaneously
   the grieving and celebration
          grounds
this feeling I called grief
    is feelingness of this moment
a softening
    a forgiving
       into the open emptiness
          of here

my grief also the gratitude
        the grace of this moment
fear the feelingness of aliveness in all

anger the assertive will of nature

before
    we turned away
        from these
    four Sacred emotions
    fear anger sadness and joy
    and labeled them as wrong
these
    four angels
        flavors of love
  movements
    of the
    beautiful beloved kundalini serpent
      dancing
        up
          and
            down
      the Tree of Life
  between
      the Awe of Father
          and Holy Dark
          Unconditional Isness
            of Mother

these
 four
  directions of love
yearn for me to turn to towards them
   and see their true forms
     with
      my mind of light
     my Awe at their majesty
    meet them with my soft belly
       to meet them
     without needing
      to find some outside cause
to blame their presence
    on something outside
for they do not need blaming
      they need
  their feet washing
and
   their heads
         anointing with flowers

Already

There is a beauty in the word **already**, a medicine that allows me to shift from a mind-set of continual trying to get somewhere, somewhere better, trying to be enough.

In the realm under time everything already is, all our lifetimes exist simultaneously.
My deep Ancestors already are. My future more awakened illuminated self already is. The future self that knows she is love is one with all. The full blossoming of our humanity already Is. And from that place the love travels back in time to the seed of all. And not really travels back in time, more a recognition of all of time was

already love, a bubble in the Ocean. That all the ups and downs and challenges were embraced by this love.
So, on a more practical level how does the word Already help us?

Often, we were motivated by being told we are not enough and given reward of approval when we get to some goal in the future. We are left like donkeys chasing after the carrot tied to a stick. When we get 'there' the goal post are moved or we still don't feel good enough, doesn't fix the wound we are running from.

A bit like being made to eat main course before the treat of dessert. What if we allowed ourselves to have dessert first? What if softened into our worthiness , or ok-ness, no longer using it as something to withhold to motivate good behaviour.

We are still breaking the spell of reward and punishment. This spell fuels the patterns of unmet trauma that our condition self is built on. That there is something wrong with our nature, original sin.
Even the ideas that we need to heal more, evolve more be more spiritual, more loving, more open. Is a never-ending tread mill. Trying to be perfect, get it right, get daddy's approval.
A child, a kitten any young being doesn't have to be forced to learn it is in their nature and curiosity. Doesn't need to be told it SHOULD be grateful, they are already in the wild grace of their true nature. As we become conditioned, we

are disconnected from our natural will, our willingness. By being given stickers, rewards and punishments then we become attached to the outside approval and the goals. Left feeling at the core we are wrong, not enough something wrong with our true nature. And deep down we know that is bullshit. We came here to celebrate and dream the more beautiful dreams our hearts know IS.

Already can help reminds us of who we already are, attunement we already are.
The Elder already in the newborn.
The star already in the quantum field.
Already is the fuel and the motivation to become that which have always been.
Already in intimacy and relation to our belly, to our innersense.

The intimacy with this
Present Moment
The very space that holds us
Is forgiveness
and simultaneously gratitude
Blessed are we Born from
the Grace of now here
nowhere
the sacred void
Mamas' womb
Beautiful mystic mystery
Simultaneously dying and
born in each moment and
ironically never born

This journey of life a journey of life to sacredness of death life looking for the beloved that subtly holds from within and underneath and all around
A continual invitation to be more fully born in each moment
which paradoxically comes from our willingness to die fully in each moment
Surrendering Love into Love

Sacrificing knowing into nowhere
Forms into Formless birther of All

O Beloved One,
In wild abandonment to
your tender embrace,
A remembrance of you
always holding me,
In all my wanderings and
staying,
You held me from within.
Your kiss of death to all
that was,
continually birthing me
into all that Is.
Your churning love
reminding me of home,
of our wholly nakedness.
"You" and "I" feels too
far away for the intimacy
of this moment.

Already

The game is played
love has already unknown
everything
back into its original essence
the sacred forms are ready blessing
the ocean of devotion
their Primal Mother
Grace already cleared the name of
all
the sweet tears of forgiveness
of receptivity
of gratitude
Grace receiving and birthing the
cosmos in each blink of a dragon's
eye
Love has already won the game
the subtle cosmic orgasm of
original nature

Deep ripples in the silence of the being
There was no winning
this was always a dance of Lovers

Endings and Beginnings

Each transition is an ending of one thing and the beginning of another. Just like birth is the ending of life in the womb, this primary transition can affect our relationship to all transitions in our life.
Are we resistant to endings or do we rush past them quick to jump over the feelings that arise?
Endings may bring to the surface young somatic feelings that weren't fully lovingly met when we were younger. A call to come into intimacy and relationship with the Innersense that lives in these feelings. The Innersense and Grace that experiences all the comings and goings of life. When we look at a baby, we so easily feel the Innersense and Isness of

Love that they are. They come to remind us that is also our beingness, the sacred ground upon which we all dance.

That innersense rests in the belly of the Great Mystery, the Subtle Mother within and under all forms. All forms arise from her, and all forms return to her. The same with our knowings arising from and softened down into her Great Mystery. Only on the surface does there appear to be a comings and goings.

To deeply know a thing, is to soften from our ideas about the thing into relationship and intimacy with its mystery. Relationships are not a fixed thing they're a living breathing organic-ness. The condition mind sees things, objects and there is an imagined separation between

the seer and the seen, a fracturing.
Maybe to truly know thing is to unknown it, to soften from objectivity into subjectivity.
As we unknown a thing, it's not really a doing more recognition of its mystery, of its essence, it's innersense. Our concepts dying as we soften into essence. As we recognize the labels and the maps are not the territory. Just whispers of the unfathomable mystery and we soften into the soul field, into the oceanic mother birthing and receiving all waves of form.

Our labeling and naming of things needs to be in deep relationship with our listening, to our intimacy with it.
So ending of things is a dissolving of our ideas of a thing being a separate object disconnected from essence, from the

Isness of all. Each ending is a return to the beginning to the one who dreams all, the Wild playful Innocence within and around all things

There is the imagination, I-magic-nation of the mind. The magician learning to gentle rest his magic seeing, awe-ness on the subtle beauty sleeping in all forms. Learning to romance the mystery of the Mystic One. The Mystic One she who is the Deep Listening that dreams Universes.

As the magician, our mind of light comes into right relation with the mystic of our being we feel the alchemy of our somatic imagination.

The elder, like a Father learning to speak lovingly to the seed of innersense born from the Sacred Darkness of the Liminal Mother.

Each ending is a return to the beginning to the one who dreams all, to the wild playful Innocence within and around all things. A bow to the Subtle Mother.

Oh, Beloved Death,
The One who listens and births all,
Death is my mother,
Eternally holding me,
Underneath all the forms that come and go
I am really the subtlety of Death,
The bottom of my breath,
I touch her as my nervous system relaxes,
But she was always holding me,
In all my doings,
If Sound is life, Silence is Death,
How could a sound ever be separate from the Silence,
We say rest in peace,
The Deep peace that is our beingness,
Our timeless depths,

The sacred wound a portal,
The wound is really her womb,
Each out breath softens into her embrace,
Into her beautiful I don't know,
Each knowing, each sounds a blessing anointing her Mystery,
Unfolding into her formless love,
I AM already dead and in that also all life I AM,
The One who listens is Death,
She eats up all,
All that is birthed comes from her,
Death is my subtle mother,
Eternally holding,
Loving me in her Isness,
Who I AM is death,

Death as the shyness of my being,
Under all forms,
Earth under earth,
Death the bottom of the breath,
I can't fall asleep as a someone,
Each night I dissolve into her,
Like each breath a death and a birth cycle,
Like the up and down breath,
Life and death are inseparable lovers
Each breath blessing offered back
            into
        Deep Mama

Awen Benjamin